ADVANCE PRAISE FOR

AUTO/BODY

"In this collection, Vértiz asks the necessary questions, invites us to give our thanks and not our judgement, and shows us that the way forward is through the memories we live out daily."

—RAQUEL SALAS RIVERA, former poet laureate of Philadelphia

"Vickie Vértiz's voice sings out like a trumpet on a battlefield. She writes with a pen so determined it could win a war. Her poems make even the most foreign parts of the world feel known and personal. What a way to ascend and take us with her."

—DARREL ALEJANDRO HOLNES, author of *Stepmotherland*

"The fierceness in *Auto/Body* does not relent, whether in its crisp memory-capture or in its attention to legacy, to present, to future in its constant ache and rift of loveliness and tumult. With undeniable power and lush clarity, Vickie Vertiz writes a path for readers to follow even when 'there's nowhere to go,' even when 'the world keeps ending,' writing with 'a love which implores all of us to act & walk the fractures.'"

—KHADIJAH QUEEN, author of *I'm So Fine*

"*Auto/Body* by Vickie Vértiz is a rebellion against violence and colonization. 'Rights to land that was never / yours Now you dig your hands into teenage girls.' Her linguistic virtuosity challenges, cajoles, and questions repressive attitudes. She playfully engages metaphor, paradox, and satire. Vértiz is a bold, strong voice. 'I'm not afraid. In this sparkle, in the middle of all of us, I am / not afraid to burn down this and every song.'"

—SHERYL LUNA, author of *Magnificent Errors*

AUTO/BODY

THE ERNEST SANDEEN PRIZE IN POETRY

Editors
Joyelle McSweeney, Orlando Menes

2023   *Auto/Body*, Vickie Vértiz

2022   *Magnificent Errors*, Sheryl Luna

2019   *Splinters Are Children of Wood*, Leia Penina Wilson

2017   *Among Ruins*, Robert Gibb

2015   *Underdays*, Martin Ott

2013   *The Yearning Feed*, Manuel Paul López

2011   *Dream Life of a Philanthropist*, Janet Kaplan

2009   *Juan Luna's Revolver*, Louisa A. Igloria

Editor
John Matthias (1997–2007)

2007   *The Curator of Silence*, Jude Nutter

2005   *Lives of the Sleepers*, Ned Balbo

2003   *Breeze*, John Latta

2001   *No Messages*, Robert Hahn

1999   *The Green Tuxedo*, Janet Holmes

1997   *True North*, Stephanie Strickland

Vickie Vértiz

AUTO/BODY

University of Notre Dame Press
Notre Dame, Indiana

University of Notre Dame Press
Notre Dame, Indiana 46556
undpress.nd.edu

Published in the United States of America

Library of Congress Control Number: 2022947713

ISBN: 978-0-268-20392-4 (Hardback)
ISBN: 978-0-268-20393-1 (Paperback)
ISBN: 978-0-268-20391-7 (WebPDF)
ISBN: 978-0-268-20394-8 (Epub)

The words are maps.
I came to see the damage that was done
and the treasures that prevail.

Adrienne Rich,
"Diving into the Wreck"

We are against what they have done and are still doing to us; and we have
something to say about the new society to be built; and we share in that
which they have sought to discredit.

Stefano Harney and Fred Moten paraphrase
C. L. R. James in "the university: last words"

Contents

Acknowledgments   ix

ALTERNATOR

nature armed medicine   5

Umbral   6

Only We Make Beautiful Things Just to Destroy Them   7

'69 Chevy Impala   9

I don't know what else to tell you about t e a r g a s   10

Anther   11

San Francisco   12

This Is the Kind of Shit I Can't Talk to Anyone About   14

God Is a Jacket Made of Tinsel   16

La Cuenta   19

George Michael at the Virgin Megastore   21

Desfile   23

Disco   24

'61 Ford Sunliner   25

I('m) a dominó, every here   26

You. Just. Can't. Kill. Us.   27

Happiness Is Going to Pieces   29

DISTRIBUTOR

I Want to Last   33

Do You Know What Time It Is?   35

La Corona   36

'70 Chevy El Camino   39

'85 Chevy El Camino   41

Caprice Classic   43

Thank You 1-800#s   44

Still—Each and Every   47

I Take—and Keep—My Flesh   48

I'm that bitch: A Voice Mail   50

Three Girls in a Subway   52

TRANSMISSION

Dictation   55

We Had to Become Doves: An American Sonnet   56

Jotería [All the things you forgot to say]   57

In College I Learned to Swim   58

Cyanotype (in a New York Public Library)   61

At 4 a.m., the radio is off   63

It Is Winter and You're No Bunny Slope   65

Overheard in a Garden   67

Here, My Photo of You   68

Mexika Hi Fem (Coatlicue Come)   69

Notes   71

Acknowledgments

I am grateful to the editors of the following books, journals, and magazines for publishing poems from this collection, at times in different forms:

Academy of American Poets, "Poem a Day" series, editor T. C. Tolbert

Boom California, Romeo Guzmán and Carribean Fragoza, eds.

Ecotone, Anna Lena Phillips Bell and Rachel Taube, eds.

The Equalizer III, Michael Schiavo, ed.

Fifth Wednesday Journal, Ana Castillo and Vern Miller, eds.

Foglifter, Dan Lau, guest ed.

Fractured Ecologies, Chad Weidner, ed.

The Los Angeles Review of Books, Callie Siskel, Poetry Editor

Nevertheless, #ShePersisted, Barbara Jane Reyes, ed.

Pleiades, Latinx Folio, Ruben Quesada, guest editor, Jenny Molberg, Editor

The Progressive, Jules Gibbs, ed.

Spillway 28, Marsha de la O and Phil Taggart, eds.

Spiral Orb 12, Eric Magrane, ed.

Voices de La Luna, James R. Adair, ed.

World Literature Today, Daniel Simon, ed.

AUTO/BODY

ALTERNATOR

nature armed medicine

&

did not

make republics, nor

relegate love to citizenship

nor property to barbarians in cities

made of cloth I reason that governments

slip behind   previous gods & will I assure you

collect regret   Laws are a gathering of claimants or

is it the sacredness of rights you wish to steel? Rights to land that was never

yours Now you dig your hands into teenage girls   but this earth watches, bides its time

to saw off your limbs You are a mockery of duty   You tried to turn occupation into limbs to

drown us, rounding up children   but we are uninterrupted   We are a thousand river

remedies   a love which implores all of us to act & walk the fractures   halt uniforms from

doing their job I've redrawn this friendship treaty, traitor. The only reason we're in your movies

is to lift the sod of your mistakes   Your life goes on   yet luck runs out   A piano will

plunge & crush your purple dahlias & lemonade   Ahora has caído y dueles   Voy a hacer

que me pidas perdón   Tú de mí no te vas a burlar   Eres como una basura En el suelo

tirado como debes amar en   tierra ajena tu hincado en muchas espinas me me me pedirás

perdón tú   tú tú que me traicionaste sin razón   Ya ves looooo que resulta Tú me hiciste tu

enemigo Brotarás sangre por mi puro capricho Aman otihuetz ihuan timococohua' Otihuetzito'

campa' miac huitzli' Itic zoquiatl   Motlacayo' aman yezquiza' & the same necessities

shall remain shall shall shall be required and on this and every day thereafter   We declare

there is more than enough for everyone. We declare that we are aware of what cannot be a body

Nor do we want one.   What cannot be a citizen is a great good thing   Treacherous and

necessary Instead—gleaned from blood—we are a Tonantzin faith of impractical limits   We

ruined your maps & so, so so, being inhabited by the worst, the most general of savages We

arm   poppies & huitzils & remind you   that   what we have is bigger than what we do

not possess   Aman quiahui' ihuan nochi' xoxhqui'. Ahora llueve y todo reverdece

Umbral

sitting in private houses, understand
the students disappeared—again—and where could they have
gone? that hour was shut, we thought, we hoped
  (¿a dónde se puede ir a esa hora?)

i thought of the silence of an onion   and of the abyss that separates
us from other abysses, vidas now cenotes, silent like money
   umbral de lengua

leemos el periódico   cerramos los ojos
y nos separa un trozo de cebolla

                      hay que cruzar
hay que cruzar o desaparecer   porque todo el mundo se esfuma
         hagamos un cielo en el infierno

Only We Make Beautiful Things
Just to Destroy Them

The Mexicans and the Russians were always in on it
This is collaboration in zero gravity democracy
—blurry violet lights and no clear answer
This is a nuclear glow in the dark so we can start over

We board planes to Mars and six engines fire
You spin away. It's candy guts out here—our voting machines are breaking
You tumble and can't stop
Grab a harness—an adult pigtail

Six motors click on and your homie has to escape
Push you so you can swing at the exploding star
A way of thinking, una estructura doblada

Alguien cortó oropel azul en cuadritos
And stuffed it into the piñata. A yellow paleta
Big as a chicken, floats to the right-hand corner and balances
Tipping into the comrade's hands

What's a layer of confetti and candy compared to DDT
The kind you sprayed over our naked bodies

We're diamonds: hard, shiny, and we can go through some shit
We don't infest, pendejo. We invest
There goes your friend again, diving toward
The paleta, which has to be pineapple

We were always in on it together
Me and my honey watching a video on loop
We gently hold each other like the beach balls we are
The light dims and that constellation swings

Only one Russian cosmonaut will smile at a time
They watch a homie swim away

Reach out
Don't make someone else do your work for you
Some of us were grounded
The whole time

'69 Chevy Impala

What I learned from my father's honking is that
women on the street are just like everyone's
mom: leggings and long T-shirts. They shoot him
dirty looks. I tell him to stop. Slink into the back seat
cover my face with my hands. We're all in the car wit
h him. Chuy repeats what I said in a whiny voice.
Our baby brother is asleep. "Watch the road, pinche
viejo," Amá says. She sucks her teeth. Sighs.
Dad laughs. Twists his mustache. He's waiting for the
green light. There's nowhere to go. I want to run out
of the car to Chris' Burgers with my friends, or the To
ys R Us on Eastern. Dad always says the same thing:
"Ponte trucha, mija. Look out." He bobs and weav
es. Punches the air. He tugs his bottom eyelid: watc
h everything. Dad can make you laugh, even when
you're mad. He's a real hit. He can get
a job, a drink, or a look, any time. You can drop him
anywhere in the world and in two days he'd have a
job and a woman to chase. He's a crooked accountant.
His math's messed up. Hides debt in too much informati
on: "Be careful," he says. "There's a lot of locos out
there." He points out to the world with his chin.
"Okay, Apá," I say. "Whatever." And I am a great stud
ent. He teaches me to look out, to give men nasty looks,
but also that fools can honk at anything in a skirt and get to drive
away. That sounds good to me: do whatever you want,
go whenever you want. And no one tells you shit.

I don't know what else to tell you
about t e a r g a s

but I am c e r t a i n it's no good for n a c h o s   Don't add extra salt to your salted-down honey. That's how those chips climb on your s h o u l d e r and stay there. It was n a t u r a l, you said   a l i t t l e c h i l e in the eye   Exactly like the chiles you put in your n a c h o s   A l i t t l e splash, a l i t t l e spray   How about we do it over your baby's e y e s? Ay como le gusta chillar a ese mocoso   In your dreams, w h o is the m o n s t e r?   Is it you, but out of u n i f o r m ? Do you wear border patrol green to y o u r f a m i l y events? Verde jalapeño V e r d e envidioso   On noche b u e n a did you ask the baby Jesus for papers?   Did they hold up a hand and tell you to fuck o f f?   When the robed baby set your boots on fire, did the flames catch your aura's e d g e s? Your protective h e l m e t ? Besides, no one eats n a c h o s before   they come to this country   This country which means y o u a n d m e   But you don't know that   You   don't know y o u r o w n f o o l self is choking on the same gas   only yours comes as a p a y c h e c k, a flat white body   Let me be c r y s t a l c l e a r: You are a rat-poison excuse for t h o u g h t   You haven't g o n e a n y w h e r e , read a n y t h i n g, s e e n anyone that didn't love cowboys   those busted a s s , b u r n e d o u t wagons   Everything is on f i r e you stupid mother fucker   Please , l i t t l e baby Jesus set these demons ablaze. Rapture these good-for-nothings. Dip them in acid—mail them in pieces to narco sidekicks who make people into hot-dogs-on-a-stick. The world keeps ending, but we're s t i l l not dead. I am all out of curses that d o n ' t also hurt m e.

Anther

After Sebastian Hernández'

Have you
noticed how the
strobe light is also
a searchlight? The same
way we are surveilled is how we
celebrate. Tinsel is our stage, our
backstage curtain. Our chreesmas leaky
ceiling bucket. Covered in gelatinous detritus, we put
things on and take them off. A harness for an automatic
pistol. A wine glass kicks its legs up. Butterfly hair clips and a
brushed-out bob. Outside it's the X-Files on the sidewalk. Inside,
there's a green neon star on your back. That shape shifts and
you do too. You keep emerging as someone else in a smoke machine flood
A sheath here to rhinestone your ____. I've been too tired to tell you, but you mean
everything to me. Your water works and projected crimson swish across a wall. What
does it cost us to make art and what is the cost if we don't? We're neighbors, Dancer.
Femmes in translucent heels, teetering on platforms of drag show leftovers. I came today
for your filament and you gave me flashing LEDs. I want you to leave me a piece of you,
the afterbirth, if you can spare it. I'm hoping to be born one more time before the world
keeps glowing. Déjame un pedacito de ti: pegajoso y fragrante, como el vello entre tus
piernas

San Francisco

Una vez estuve por encima del mar
Extraña en mi vestido de pétalos grises
Me pesa este ramo de tiempo
Este sueño de petate

No siempre vivo en lo roto
Una vez bailé
Bajo neón verde
Gay con gorditas, mujeres
Que conozco bien
Cumbiamos en la niebla
Hasta las nahui
Nos clavamos bajo las olas
Que baile
Que tapdance ni que chiquihuite

Nunca he nadado
Pero el hielo está en todas partes
La gente se dobla y hierven la sal
Gaviotas frotan salobre en sus poros
Entre mis ojos de papaya guardo
El tipo angular
Contra la sal, mi boca
Mi nariz: a pesar del desprecio
Son para ti, para la alegría del mundo

Mis aletas son campos de arroz
Me impiden montar mi bicicleta
Eres mi abrigo de pieles necesarias

Y así duermo
con los ojos abiertos
Como un tiburón

This Is the Kind of Shit I Can't
Talk to Anyone About

We must have already been naked, looked out at the gold

Hills and said, We need to kiss next to all of that

Nos fuimos afuerita on the yellow grass

It was warm. Hacía sol. Maybe you convinced me

Or I, you. Nos pegó no sé que

But what if someone sees us, the eternal

Question that keeps me from myself. But everyone already knows

So we opened the French doors, crawled carefully out

Covered the floor with someone else's blanket

Your hair, too, was long and brown

And your breath was sweet water so I kissed you

The hawks above unimpressed

With our throbbing, but they could see I loved you

And your breasts, well, I knew they were not for me

Forever, and because I knew what you liked, I did it, just

More slowly because we were outside on a field trip

And because I was hungry I ate and ate

All I do is take, take, take, you said

So I took and took and took you

Rode and rode and rode you

(Maybe I was not doing anything new)

And I surprised myself. I pleaded: bend,

flip, rearrange me

And I loved it like that. Like that sun on us—a dying

star, everywhere at once

God Is a Jacket Made of Tinsel

I'm looking at your amen
A strobe tenderness, a lucky silver

...

You are a chimera
Your lover's ex-wife says this. This about what she doesn't see
in you. But how could she?
She'd have to admit that she is twine and not
the tinsel you are

...

And where will you end up if you keep following a ghost?
He doesn't stay, but he keeps coming back

...

Three men tried to rearrange your face with tape, men drag-
ging you into their truck. Another alley, another day of life

...

Perhaps it has been a month of tears
May Archangel Rafael walk you home, his feathers bruised camellias
on the sidewalk, a gilded miracle crossing

You felt yourself, found yourself
In your own lap
It is not strange. That is where mirrors belong

...

You gave some guy a languid blowjob because. Because
That's on the menu if a femme chooses it in grief

...

I'm going to survive, you said and flew, up
Past and through the ceiling to the light

The one Pat Cleveland is always talking about—the catwalk light:
Oh you just want to dance and play and leap and gosh

It's just like heaven
All those hands lifting you higher

...

In this beat there is something else—a request
Get off. Bájate cabrón que tengo una emergencia: get off
So I can be a vessel for peace. Let me be love, you say

Let me be the mariposeo of spider eyelashes
Swooping up and into the screen. A woman

In this beat, a rapture of sticky floor,
In this beat, a licking whisper
In this beat we're pinwheels

For her, our bodies turn into bridges, that open
or close for passing boats
Scissor the air, ticker tape sisters

Your ghost hologram across the room, to whom
you close your eyes to

...

You have danced us into a new religion: a party like yourself appearing
A fantastic god and their tinsel sweeping

La Cuenta

You flash me a smile
Una sonrisita sin motivo, sin explicación
You twirl in your leather jacket—the fringe
Grazes my arm. That is the distance from which I love you
There are too many people to share you with
What am I supposed to do?

A little here, a little there
I am only as good
as the worst of our people

Ya tengo mi tesoro en nuestro amor
I'll order your dresses, white satin capes that tie at the waist
I'll count and recount the money
I can do it, I can do it well
A couple of times, you've held my hand
Your Coty powder is my skin
But there are so many people to share you with
What am I supposed to do?

A little here, a little there
You are only as good
as the worst of your people

I'll iron your diamonds—estos son los tiempos que guardo yo
In the moonlight, my ring is a flash of silver in your hand
I breathe into your shine but can't keep living like this, I can't
time my love bomb in different little tiempos. So it went off
The total came in through my moonroof, my todos tiempos
Me: the No in the Yo. I can't love different than me
I'm not enough moonstone
Me: I'm the little room

George Michael at the Virgin Megastore

I saw him from a listening station
When I turned toward the descending stairs

There he was: head-to-toe white
A shadowed cheek
His linen billowed—the finer things some of us want

I can't tell what's true
from what I have seen
Harmless deception it keeps things this way

Behind him an iridescent cd aura, sunlight through the glass
A brief saxophone solo started in my ears
It was George and I didn't ask him to sign anything

I didn't say hello. What could I ask him, my tapes
Of his were in a box under my bed
My white shorts walked out of the store

Into the parking lot, which was any city with movie stars
My heart ran fast into my friend's car
Ran down Sunset until it became Brooklyn

I kept running until I was ready
To look into another kind of light
I am still running

And I run into a Jack-in-the-Box bathroom
Above me a pearled fluorescence
Mom and I had just left the doctor's

So there must've been hot pink syrup in her purse
As I washed my hands, a light opened the door
It was her: Amá in white

Cotton pants and a yellow polo
She said, *I can't work any harder than I do*
I don't know what the hell you want me from me, oh

My mom sings. My breath
My breath here is suspended because what can you say to that?
I'm sorry I don't help you, mami. I'm spoiled and I dried my hands

Or maybe I said, *Ay Amá* and laughed
And if I did, she definitely smacked me in the face
So pretty much what I said was going to show regret or keep it moving

But I didn't run. I couldn't. Where do you go when you're too small
When you can't help your mom the way you want to: pay for jet planes to escape a
Cheating lover, holiday getaways to snowy mountains

I could stay by her side. So we
Walked—definitely glided toward the bus
Past the wonton warehouses
The green lawns of commerce
Back to our neighborhood of descending bus stops—
We were head-to-toe fine shadows
Another kind of light

Desfile

After the 2018 Mexican Independence Day Parade in East Los Ángeles

How long have you been holding this flag? Can you tell us in French? In the
Mexican language? Qué bonito tener México aquí. Come see the 71st year of the
Mexican Independence Day Parade (in Los Angeles). Even the Junior ROTC is here,
especially the Junior ROTC: disciplined children with empty rifles. A white anchor's
on the street.   *Viva México* says the Azteca, and he throws in a
Viva America like it's a different place. Like it's not here, and
can you call those tires? On a lowrider—is that the right
word? We are so loyal, like the Junior ROTC because the
devil gave us a GI Bill once. Compton cowboys gallop just
a   little because it's 95 degrees out here, Celsio. So
pinche hot,   but everyone is so *joyeux* to be out here in
front of the dentist's office,   then the bus stop, then la Clínica de
los Doctores. People   are representing Puebla, but they
don't have costumes, is that   the right word? "People"?
Wave very slowly, princess—don't beak   a sweat, don't
break a sweat, don't brick a swat. Ms. México
National, what a silhouette, como pastel de quinceañera. I feel
like I'm part of the community, says the pocha anchor, and she is—look
at those rims, is the hood lifting off? The Buick is leaning
to the right. Just how do they do that? Lift off

and wave at the same time? Ride and drive and *le geste*. Work and work and
drive and work at the same time. It is the *ancient habit* of my people—
electric rose acrylic and platinum pinstripes. We feast on tongue
and doubt. *Imbeciles* and invoices. Bones and myrrh.
Your *sirènes* and *entrailles*.

Disco

One Saturday night, Mario takes me to Circus Disco. Our path is a
smoke trail of bacon-wrapped hot dogs. We're really not on a date. His
muscle tank top is ribbed tight. All eyes are on him. *Como copo de algodón,*
ay la verdolaga. He spins me into the riot: men opening fast — cumbia hinges.
Bodies perfumed in high cinnamon and cool water eye scream. Some women
wear button-ups and newsboys, others tacones and red enamel. The lights go out
and Rocío Dúrcal walks into the spotlight. She drifts in an emerald dress. Her neck
is rhinestone vibrato. This is my first drag show and I don't know the rules. Rocío
sings: Me gustas mucho. Me gustas mucho tú. Middle-aged men and señoras who
look like my mom hold up dollars. Look at us, just regular degular. We swoon and
snap when Rocío takes them. A kiss and another on her cheek. Her lips quiver.
The room alight with splendor—sequins and khakis, tight black skirts and
hungry paychecks. Then my brain makes the record skip—a bald dude in a
Dodgers Jersey walks up to her. Who is this fool? I say Girl, Mario says. Don't
you know everyone has a dollar? The homie gently tucks the bill in the
gemstone bosom. Shit, I think. If he can be gay, he who probably drives a
Caprice Classic, or maybe a Honda Civic with a loud loud tailpipe—if his
bald head can be gay, then so can I. I can be a cumbia riot. I'm not a player
like some fools but I can be hot pants and Rocio's lipstick. I'm saying I
want to be an emerald bosom. Go, Dodgers! Play ball. Play me Love is the
Message and I'll learn how to hustle, how to push my hips so far I'll knock
fools down. I'm not afraid. In this sparkle, in the middle of all of us, I am
not afraid to burn down this and every song. Did I find my light? Is
there one for me? Is this the moon, or am I just born?

'61 Ford Sunliner

I was once a Tristar vehicle .   Who procured my mettle   ?   My pilot bears
the springs   .   The body-on rear-view   .   Who revved my
transmission canary yellow   ?   I toiled until I didn't   .   The gaskets
blowing this cover, this trunk try   .   He will ignore my failing rack and pinion
          .   He's already staring at another Galaxy , the chrome so clean   He
think he can see himself   .
When they put a sign in my back window   ,   I won't be down and glittered blue
          .   Any passenger can steer   .   I am watching for automatic
restoration   .   Looking for a replacement carriage   ,   a mother, a maker
          .   Mine was a near-solid gasket ,   my original model   .   She
hopped in a Chevy so fast, my driver barely knew she was gone   .   Who can resist
a mustache like that.   I could be his first   ,   I won't be his last
          .   I had a body before,   before it was gone forever   .

25

I('m) a dominó, every here

gray and bare
not bird or bush

I plait,
ill, ma(')
round and up
es(a) ros(a) está rota
, p_to
(s)he's lovely
(a) long wild wound
the wound, the ground
a tall potion

I laced a tense, see
the wild es sí
and round it was
up, on a hill
(a) long wild wound
I'll rose up and raw around
no longer wound f(oo')
not a bird or brush
like nothing else in tense, ése

You. Just. Can't. Kill. Us.

This earthquake was my fault. It's my birthday and this is what happens. Watch the videos of the patria swaying, then collapsing. My earthquake trap is a lime stain pretending to be hands. The metro Rosario is the inside of a tooth. Cuba keeps winning with the lowest death toll in the hurricane Olympics—so much hunger, so many games. This tunnel is damp earth and petroleum. Dinosaurs and roses. What did we do to deserve eight long thrashing points. The saints are pulling up their silky skirts, rubbing their long eyelashes so hard that they fall off. The aftershocks continue, los derrumbes tambien. To entertain myself I do all the accents I know: Blanche Deveraux, Rose Nylon, Sofia. Picture it: we light the matches in our pockets, every hero on a train has them. The biggest thief there is—the president, a real raptor with spoons for lips. I can't wait to see the homemade videos of the patria swaying, then collapsing. Towers of chilaquiles. If the buildings don't kill us, then the hipsters will. If the Mexican poets see you in a huipil, it's over. This isn't going to be good enough. We have to do it ourselves. Take a pick ax and dig. And in Oaxaca all the muxes are already rebuilding the isthmus. On the floor above, no one is coming to save us. How do you say "they" in Spanish? I want to break into pronouns. I'll tell them it's my birthday and do they have a cake, petroleum, or rositas. But someone does come. And the hands are passing me overhead, a mosh pit at the apocalypse. These men I'm not supposed to look at carry me, carry the passengers. When I'm let down the earth is still shaking, so I jump over the fissures in the earth that nothing can fill. I know that kind of hole. Yellow apartments tip over like a drunk señora on her birthday bender, her sisters catch her by the arms. Some things still stand. Soon Puerto Rico still won't have water, still won't have electricity. And now do you see being a colony is not so great? It's not their fault the president is still down there in the dark and sometimes he's the most beautiful chicken asshole in the world if he's not trying to kill you. And if the smog didn't kill us, then the sugar will. Take a pick ax and dig. And wouldn't you know: the rubble is not a grave but a great motor. Our ground still trembles but I am up to walk home. I'll just have to tunnel through. The earthquake was my fault but there are too many tremendous disasters to keep track of all the little ones. I get there and Puerto Rico still doesn't have electricity but our president's in jail. He begged us to shoot him, but we reconsidered. He pissed himself and now it's raining. My cousin still thinks my Spanish sucks. Did I forget to do my spelling homework? Se va a caer! The tower of homework, balancing on a rotten apple anyway. Fire in my pocket and it's not independence day. Our president has lips like a chicken's culo. I may stay down in the dark even if they come and get me. Here I thought it was already crushed. If the falling buildings don't kill you, the smog will. If the smog doesn't, the boy in a truck might. But when we are outside, the sum of us warms us. The sun touches parts no one can. You. Just. Can't. Kill. Us. If. The. Earth. Can. Not.

Happiness Is Going to Pieces

After Victor Estrada's sculpture, Happiness

Tell me about balance. And how you hold it and Boyle Heights
The weight of night jasmine which smells like death
& a brother who made you read *¡Alarma!* to him
because he could not read Spanish

We have our languages, and then we don't
Our people win ultramarathons without a major sponsor. In huaraches
Born to run. We can't run fast enough away from malevolent patrols
and toward indictments that never arrive

I don't try to catch you, but I stay
close enough to know I am not lost. I have assembled
these objects in your honor: a slow hamstring stretch—
the science of not tipping over. Pearls, cholesterol.

Your stride is industrial-sized, a long-distance confidence
I do not wonder about your resolve
It explains your collections of dust motes
and Coach wallets. Started from the bottom
now we have two hybrids and read Vanity Fair
Four fat couches in your living room
but not enough place settings for more than three guests

Show me the previews and coming attractions
Will we still have to do a lot of back-seat fucking
with funky spunk?
My back's not strong enough for that

Happy birthday. Happy cotton candy instead of popcorn
I got you a side-eye cat and
you don't want it, I know
You will outrun it all and I don't blame you: who wants
to be green in the face, your arms in your ears—your eyes
bugging out, Martin and Gina fighting in the living room
No. Forget that
Follow your skinny legs
and fly

DISTRIBUTOR

I Want to Last

Like a dark star

Be the feature in your marine sky

A coming attraction

Never mind your knees

Forget the owl that circles

She is I

Much too available

Hunting: Clutching her cell phone

Unlimited: texting. Things I cannot say.

But I will:

I don't normally sweat anyone this hard

I am an owl, after all

And the afterlife is a mighty long time

My claws hold the bar steady

I do not sleep when you do

My night is the opposite of rest. I dream

we walk into a barn together, outstretch

our wings and sweep out

all we do not need: _____

My dream, my loving is a fern

Uncoiled some days, a fractal the rest

Primordial *as lust*. And older.

On your next birthday, we will *stretch our brief bodies*

Into a *rage of waves* and no longer

wrecked with hunger

Do You Know What Time It Is?

After the photograph Candy Cigarette *by Sally Mann and the protest-performance organized by Cherríe Moraga and Celia Herrera Rodriguez with the nonprofit Al Otro Lado at the Otay Mesa Detention Center*

I always do   They sell candy crack pipes at the liquor store—where have you been?

                I used to be safe and

sage among the wolves   Now this cage is too small

And I move to live   So when I dream, I necklace storied playgrounds

Under a pebble roll of clouds   I am a doe like a doe is a buck   Horns sprout

through my skull   I open one door   slide open another, then

another and it's just empty warehouses   Piled high with Mylar blankets

        We're not the only ones running a marathon

And these mornings   The sky is a blue that hurts   A rectangle sky from

a balcony I can't see over   I see through it   We've been falling

from that sky forever   These mornings, when I leap   Women in

white drum and weep   I leap and evening flies

La Corona

"We have been at war with the crown for at least 500 years."
—Celia Herrera Rodriguez

I.

I come from a long line of glass green queens

My godmother: reyna del paper cut pueblo
Her daughter is a long night terror
Puro chisme iridescence
They're far-away reinas we keep a mean distance from

Amá wasn't a queen but she sharpens eyeliner with
Razor blades. The duchess of slaughter

Me? I'm a fake princess—I'd rather be Amá's blade
My cheeks of around midnight

We still think talking shit will make our lives sing
We're each other's evil stepsisters, that part of the psyche
That cracks two-faced cabronas into broken mirrors

II.

Como eres cabrona, Margaret
The Queen's English is
All our torturer, not just yours
¿Crees que a tu hermana le gusta seguir las reglas al pie de la letra?
Ay she does love to follow the rules
I will not defend her. They're taking her image down
everywhere now, y que bueno

We're living in three dimensions, your Highness, your high ness
You and me are *living in the shadow of the Mission*
Chicotazos some days, ball gowns another, our tongues trimmed
Washed out and dried the next

Every time you wanna look away, reinita, look in here
See over it, see it over
¿Qué te cuesta?

You're mad because your novio is trash and because you don't have a job
You're mad that you didn't win
And it wasn't even a contest, girl, you were just
born second

III.

One night Amá wanted to crown me for Halloween
I was eleven. She newspapered the floor and cut tears into paper

She would knight me into royalty. I pictured one thing, she made another
My paper crown was a tendon, a rhinestone tipped and fitted
I was Amá's poster board, the glued glitter
Where the medicine holds it all together

IV.

Margaret, ya casi ni saludas. Your sister just had her third baby
And your ass walks in like it's lunchtime
Is this why New England is so cold?
British warmth is about as hot as my huaraches in a Berkshire winter

That's royal sisters, I guess. Así se llevan
Some of us, though, are still digging
our sisters
out of the rubble that is our fathers
Your broken ass empire

V.

The crown she made wasn't what I wanted. Not metal
enough. Too much like a pueblo
I wore it in a Polaroid
Walking home from school, I blistered
In jelly heels. It's not that far in tulle

I wish I could have known how to get
between disappointment and language
How to know feelings were a two-way mirror, a test
That I could pass
How do I let my thanks,
and not my judgment, be
what I give away?

'70 Chevy El Camino

The men inside the Pep Boys wear blue work shirts. Fingerprints on the hems. That's
how I'm going to be: my hands with grease that won't wash off. Like Apá buying Freon.
Fenders. My sister sniffs the little trees, outlines the posing girls with her eyes. We buy
peanuts and their candy turns our palms to red

I follow Apá and remember 1530, the number on the oil, for when I'm older
Men fix cars and that will be me. Like this, son. Apá showed me later
Took a wrench and made it click. Twisted the bolt through the rim, and like that
we have new tires. He tests the headlights

He wants to see where we're going. But he's not done
Apá sucks his teeth. Hijodelachinagadas
drops a screwdriver. Amá brings him orange Kool-Aid and he leaves
fingerprints on the cup's plastic neck
My sister holds the flashlight for him

It's dark when the moths come
and leave their dust. I hand him tools like Operation
Not that one, Jesús, he says. The one with the magnetic tip
No. Beat it, he tells Amá. She distracts him. Bothers like a fly

And when she walks away, he flings a word at her, a wrench, hard
into his toolbox. It sounds like a tooth when it cracks
I check my teeth
They're okay, just a little big for my mouth

Tiny pebbles stick to my knees when I get up. And I think
That's not how I want to be a man. I go inside to see if I can find
That tool Apá needs to fix our car
One that can help him make it run, be more beautiful
Instead of taking it apart

'85 Chevy El Camino

After Rose B. Simpson's "Maria" in honor of artist Maria Martinez

I'm a bad bitch of high gloss
and matte juxtaposition
My body is the decolonized, sustainable thing

::   ::   ::   ::

You drive me when the world ends
And what will you wear? Other beings'
Skins: O-rings and leather. Stay strapped

A tiny wooden spear through the nose and a hoodie
Those trenzas bien peinadas
Black paint across the eyes so you can

See like a fly through goggles, block out
The new plastic possibilities
My driver made a software of suede

Across the cheek. Strung beads
Against mal de ojo, for beauty, against forgetting

::   ::   ::   ::

Este camino goes low and slow
Las manos delicadas, dedicadas juntan
Las Tres Marias

Across the corn field
Smaller hands collect squash
Pile them on my back

::   ::   ::   ::

I came out to stay out
My engine wakes the dead
Under every school

What songs do we have for them?
Masatl. Mayahuel. Jaguar. Xilonen
Heartbeats and revenge in every step

Rocks in my tire grooves. They are ancestors too
My dials tune in nopales
Makes me wanna cry

My spirit: horsepower
What I'm doing is serious. I've refinished the directions.
Take what's there and forge it into something else

Caprice Classic

Is it talking dirty if you're just listening? What you see in the picture is me riding shotgun. A cinder block wall behind me. I mailed the photo to my Romanian pen pal, me making a sexy face in my friend's Falcon. To my right is the dustless dashboard. In the backseat is my older friend Junior. Give me a sexy look, he says. He's taking a picture for my pen pal but it's really for him. It's also for me. For my other friend who's driving. My sexy hair looks like this: a ponytail on top of my head, wavy brown cascading over to the side of my face. In my denim jacket and white button up, the other thing that sizzles is my plaid flannel skirt, one my mother made. Her hands lined my hem. The driver rolls carefully up my alley. Me, trying out my sexy and he's looking too. We enjoy it, watching me try. I enjoy trying. I shelve my looks for the receiver—on the phone later, I will listen to Junior's dream in which I was giving him head under a restaurant table, the table cloth covered me and no one could see. I will play along in the dark under a blanket when everyone's asleep because he doesn't scare me. He's got skater hair, crooked teeth, and likes the Golden Girls as much as me. He drives a Caprice Classic—a mid-80s machine the color of sour wine. Oh yeah? I tell him. And then what did I do? Is it dirty if it was safe? We could turn it on—we could turn it off. He taught me how to drive that thing. Down the Commerce streets—gray warehouses and no workers inside them at night. Entire fields of pavement for us to play on. Another night, I took a fruit roll up and wrapped it around his finger, my first blowjob. Thank god his hands were clean. He was older but not older-gross just old enough to make it fun. There are infinite degrees of desire when you're 15. The mint-satin-dress quinceañera kind. The kind where all you had to do was put your head in the lap of a boy who loved you so much he could cry (and did). The kind that drives you to the drive-in and tests the limits of your high-waisted panties. The kind where you're just trying to get to school and you know you're being followed. But that's not sexy, that's surviving. That's an open secret. Junior knew my secrets: that I really loved _____ and that my friends were sometimes shitty, but also, a veces: my lovers

Thank You 1-800#s

As if making out with me because we both liked Def Leppard
Was any kind of violence

I am watching myself 20 years ago with this guy
My brother's friend who giggled with some small revenge against who knows who

I sat up in the passenger seat having just woken up
From floating in cough syrup, speed and bloody—how a panic

Attack feels like, the first time, your heart certain it will seize
and kill you—and though I wasn't dead I was thinking about it

I was only messing around with my brother's friend because I didn't have a car
(That's mean. And only half true.) He was more cinnamon than milk

A little bit of a rocker-frayed rose patches and denim elbows
He was trying to be funny, though he was shirtless and bird chested

Put a shirt on and drive? I asked and he abided
He drove us around the perimeter of our ancestral lands—

Paramount, Whittier, East LA—to cheer me up
I kept kissing him to forget what a mess I was leaving for my brother to clean up

Because of course (of course!) I would leave him
But before I mailed that letter, the rocker—who easily weighed just a bag of feathers—
Gave me a stack of blue plastic mix tapes. He drove me for so long that I could see my life
would be worth living, if only I could keep driving at night like that

In the tangerine street light, passing through the perfume of gas stations
Welling up the tank with tears. My life did not have to be razors in coat pockets
Or maneuvering slowly around innocent shaving blades left on the ledge
Of our pantry shelf, next to the microwave
Where many years later, baby cockroaches will emerge from the vents inside
Right before I put the lid on your plate of beans
And I will bring down my fist over their whole ass bodies
Even though I meditate now and shit, wishing loving kindness on all beings
All beings except these motherfuckers who are liars in life and death

There are lives and there are lies

We don't go that far, me and the rocker. After he'd told me that joke, I should've known it was over. But I turned to face him and remembered that my body was capable of more than only mending my mother's ribbons of grief

Beneath my flesh-charade was my actual heart, which the rocker enjoyed
His tiny white teeth were sweet and so was how he helped his dad with his tire business
Thank you, driver, for helping me through a death wish, bow-tied in Christmas

The day before, I had climbed all over the furniture in my mom's living room
As I talked to the suicide hotline people at my university

Thank you, 1-800#s. The voice on the other line said I would be OK
That it was normal to be deathly disconsolate that my mom

Was in always in somekindof danger. That it was triste she had to fight off her own husband
They didn't say that last part, but my heart felt ___ as if they had. So, I took a breath because

They could see the slits in our fabric, that I wasn't crazy for feeling. One foot in front of the other, I crawled across the ceiling and back onto the couch

When the sun set that day, the rocker came by in his gray Honda
and I looked at his hands again: with relief and a little bit of rain

Still—Each and Every

O, Holmes, my
Trés woods men
Every lad is a pen
Every turn is a fool

A robe hung our tribes
And we scribes had nothing else to do
But rite rite rite

So we used the
Ink, the cups
More pens, more drinks
Till—we could
, stand—
Still—each and every one:
A blade

I Take—and Keep—My Flesh

I think my friend is in love

His candy shell Falcon, a '65
Is red retro—an old romantic
My, that hurts
The Beatles grip a rage, glowing
in my throat—a lighthouse in the daytime
My friend is used to handsome alleys

I am a passenger, my leather
a crashing view
Silent streets remember
Lap belt marks on my thighs
And while I am
not my mother, I am
her skin
I am this door
Its candy apple stripe and so much steal

A dashboard burns anything
It wants you to think

This friend's car
is my ride home

We are gelled-down
and pat friends
I fall out his door
Thanks, I say into my brushed denim

Jaws clutched.
My skirt curls away from the
freeway sun.

Talk to me
Talk because
a chain-linked high
is hard on the knees

And though he's used to ignitions
I burn. We are
friends and gasoline
Should my driver four my body
and make me half, tell Amá he
crooned me, this racer, his ride
I'm sitting in

The Falcon is parking
his claws careful and far from my tips
He leans into my hot looks and where
he's darker, a pimple was once picked
He's drunk-out in love
And yet this lap is alive—backed into the seats, I take
and keep
my flesh

I'm that bitch: A Voice Mail

"I wanted The Notebook *experience, and I was getting a Post-It."*
Drag Queen Vanessa Vanjie Mateo

Hay, Vanjie girl, you are that bitch, did you know that? And who is this? Just me. I love you because you're real. IRL and on TV you're the same bitch, and so am I. We wear our hearts on our corsets. Smile when you read a girl. Your heart is fuchsia feathers and finger waves, lace up high heels and a black leather jacket, eyeliner you can kill a motherfucker with. Don't let anybody tell you what you can and can't have. Is that in *The fucking Notebook*?

And no, you don't need to know what the fuck a stirrup is, because why? Why would you know? You were born right after we stopped wearing stirrups on our leggings. So also you don't have to know who the fuck Meryl Streep is, either. She doesn't know you. Fair is fair, Billie Jean (if you don't know her either, don't trip. She's cool and unreal). And you know what else you don't need? A broke-ass ballerina from the north to love you. What about the north, Queen?

I got your notebook romance right here, girl. You fuck with *War and Peace*, though? Me neither. You like *Borderlands*? We gotta review mestizaje, did you know some eugenics fool wrote that? I know! That shit is wild. We can make up a whole way of thinking this that and the third. For real unreal. What're your favorite books? The ones from when you were little? That's dope. I'm writing you this letter. It's a missive, see, another word for "I miss you." You don't have to be from New York to be hood. You could be from Tampa and La Isla del Encanto. Where do I stay? Wherever I can hold your purse, boo. You like dick though so I gotta buy one, I know that's real.

In the future life of you and me, you only work when you want to. And we own a puppy named Mango and a villa, you and me in Miami right there, high up where the ocean won't drink us when the ice caps melt. And girl, whatever happened in *The Notebook* anyway that you want so bad? I haven't watched it, so tell me, girl, what do you want? What do you want to do to me?

Some motherfucker asked me that once and I was like, fool, what? So I kissed him hard and shit because what else was I going to say? "I don't know, suck your dick?" I'd only ever seen maybe a few pornos then and they weren't wild. I had no imagination, girl. No cookies either.

But I got cookies now, though. Help me write our own notebook, then. Is it Hieroglyphics of us fucking? You're gonna have to show me how to do the splits. What happens when we move in together, though, and we have to take out the trash? I hate the trash. Or the dishes get dirty and ain't nobody trying to clean them? What's *The Notebook* say about that? Oh, it doesn't? Let's get a dishwasher then. I can love you to death, Miss Vanjie. Don't ever let me go.

Three Girls in a Subway

Motion glows in our glass and we ride the train
And although childhoods are for first-world countries

We won't get lost
I keep you close
Bamboo earrings at least two pairs
Zipped up hoodies, friends like love, close to the scalp
Metal eaves on bird house vines

What's in the dark is why you stopped talking to me
Maybe I took up too much space. Or not enough

We're enough, I know because someone just texted me
You know what stop we're taking
So
We're enough and I know
Because someone
Just reminded me
Wherever we meet is home
One—nothing—without the other

We are so much more
Than third rail death and thunder

It is possible to be still, sister
When motion lurches us into fire
bombs—into becoming

TRANSMISSION

Dictation

The INS came to our house. Our house was built in a 1980s suburb. The outside was painted a brown beige. It was two stories, so you know it was a dream. And because there were no other houses, I let the INS officers in. And because I call them eye-en-ness you know this is in the past, but it's here again and again and again, just with new names. The Anus officers had wives. One of them had brown hair and bangs, a short haircut, a street bob. The Antennas officers didn't say anything. They were dressed like sheriffs, deputies: olive slacks and light beige shirts, aviators. They hid their eyes. They stood around the kitchen and said nothing. One of their wives, I asked her to have a seat. Or maybe she just took a seat. You know how those people are. And I knew I had to feed her, feed them, after all they were our guests. And we knew that they were there to take my brother Jesus, though he was born here. And because we were expecting the Ay-and-yes to come, Chuy had gone to hide in his black Mustang, his old one, the '92. And he was sitting in his car, hiding in the garage. He was in the dark, in plain sight for we who can see. He sat in his car for hours and hours, waiting for our guests to leave. I must have served sandwiches, the kind with the crust cut off, but that's not the kind of food we make. They were polite, tight-lipped, light-skinned. One of them had a thick accent and a high and tight buzzzz. He cut it himself with a chainsaw. He was mad at me for making him drive down the mountain. Can't you read? He said. You are trespassing. It is posted in English and Spanish. What language do you speak?

Well, I said, All of them.

Chuy waited so long that he turned into a Mustang. A workhorse, especially on Sundays. And so they finally left, bellies full of silence. Next time, said my lover, we don't have to let them in.

We Had to Become Doves: An American Sonnet

For Shirin Neshat

I am so sorry that you cannot return. Distance has been coachwhip snakes,
     slithering along a creek. I had to leave home to see it, too, to see my body, the
garments I was wearing. Education and her dangers: new words, the epistemology
     of survival as privilege. It is not one or the other. But you and I get to see from afar,
taste the pistachio of the past, wash our hands with the rose water of our present, distilled &
     something we can carry. In your dreams, Mexico stands in for Iran. Morocco is the
understudy for Algiers. For us, LA is perhaps Tehran. Honduras. Pupusas
     are not the same as gorditas. Baleadas are not quesadillas, don't even try it. We know
what it's like to be kept out by missile necklaces and barbed paperwork. By men
     fatigued with because-I-said-so-s. We had to become owls to properly hunt and drop
remedies from freeway overpasses. Our feathers are still mechanical. Sometimes
     home is inside and cannot, will not, could not be taken away. Let's fold our wings into
boats, unafraid of the sun. We are ready to burn. We tried smashing into the waves. We had to
learn to float. *Some days we commune with the moon*. Some nights, we trade secrets with the
     stag. I'm the girl folding her white wings into a plastic bag. Your imagination and the
place where two rivers meet is home. Is the ink on your hands and mine. Let us greet the sun
where our genders are miles of rattlesnakes cultivating venom. There is the shore where we
     push the boat out to sea. We too were left on the land, watching our daughters float
away. We fill our fangs with antidotes. Shoot prayers with a shell. Femme bodies slip into
     secrets and oaks. The otherwise is where we planted ourselves and grew thousands
and thousands of branches

Jotería [All the things you forgot to say]

What is hidden from the wise and good

Painting: "Atekokolli," by Gabriela M. Zapata. A brown child announces ceremony.	A sweet glitch at Monet's pond. Iztalcihuatl wants her muscles back.	A child walks up and leans on your legs, like you are hers.	The sky in the river is more azure than the real thing.
The YouTube show "La Más Draga" is a Mexican version of RuPaul's Drag Race. It's unclear what they're competing for. What's extraordinary: that the show exists at all.	The white hostess isn't queer and takes liberties with vocabulary: "Aquí ando en esta jotería" referring to her skin-tight dress, herself, or the company she keeps. ¿Qué te parece?	The drag queens are tiny, or tall, with soft beards and thick lashes. They just started or they've been doing it forever. One is basically a woodland faery and a judge calls her Poli Poquet.	Inside my cell phone hi I say: I'm waiting for a woman to love me. Someone else's phone responds: You shouldn't have to wait for anyone.
True. People forget that Mexicans look all kinds of ways: Black. Rich. Middle Class White. Fascist. Draga. Performance artist and elote vendor. Stop fucking forgetting.	Pandas are still tumbling down the slide at the zoológico de Chapultepec.	I dressed up like Dorothy Zbornak. She looked me up and down and said, "Not bad."	Calm down, New Mestiza.
My sister is terrified of earthquakes. My nieces send me paintings of red-pink daisies. But the last pintura is shades of black and says: SAD.	What does being queer look like from middle age? a. Watching myself on the Internet b. Not seeing myself c. Watching younger people recreate consent	Pop's multiple choice: a. "Do as I say, not as I do." b. "Trucha." c. "I am the monster we are all looking for" d. What about the things you cannot say?	The show's hostess isn't queer but is so rich and güera that she doesn't have to care.
True or false? An authentic Mexican is: An Aztec Cookie or a white nationalist lie.	Even elision makes a sound.	One queen paints her eyebrows into a horizon of spikes. Yo me sentí muy perra.	Hay que tener maña. Y yo, soy mañosa.

In College I Learned to Swim

To graduate gradually   And just because you can't swim doesn't mean you're dead
Just because you're dead does not make for death   Death is a president whose job it is to parent
A parent lying beneath their child, or depending on how   You look at them, a child on his
shoulders

/

How can you plan another party or play   when the saints come marching in?   What will
people say about   suitcases in the alley at night?   About whose fault it is that that baby
is gone?   And somehow we thought   It ends here. Though we've been swimming
Since water

/

I tried calling for help   But my brother signal is terrible in here   All we had to do
was stand up. Not once but as soon as we found out   The sea still tastes the brine, the one
I nearly drowned my love in   She loved to swim, to graduate
in the silt. We panicked in a reef   Shin across a shell   The scar is gone though me and you
keep

/

What keeps you warm sometimes   is that the nerve gas never touched me, such a small
consolation   when no one is calling   Don't show the drowned baby in your water again
Unless you're going   to put your fucking body down to bring her back

/

Why play the saints come marching in when the saints are   a saint already. It's like me
writing a ____ and calling it a poem   Por el amor de Dios abre la boca
We end this tonight though we are so disconnected. I push away   & exhausted from trying not
to die. Inside   my lungs, death is   another photo of a
wound   To the killer, it's only   "You shouldn't" "They should have"
All around us a sheathed   eulogy for fathers   I'm sorry is all I have

/

What is gone that was not meant for me   Honking at women like pigeons you only
want to maim

/

And because this is laden with shanks   Because here, the girl jumps up and stabs
the giant motherfucker in the eye   There are no more tomorrows of children shriveling from
your regret   No more, cabrón

/

For   Synchronization, press 3
For the operator press 2   To speak to a counselor press 0
But the insurance keeps my mom from   her counseling appointments, three and four calls
in
and we'll just have to cry into our huevos until when

/

It ends with us, driving away   Here, where we waited too long
Here, where the salt is up to our eyes   and everything we cannot reach

/

You, my sacrifice at the pyramid of the sun   Where that star sets, exactly at the top, during
summer and winter solstice   Teotihuacan belongs to its people, not just the Aztecs   We,
those unruly neighbors with chainsaw feathers and open mics

/

We had to walk a long way for this. 52 weeks of coral neon clouds   It took a Tex-Mex
minute, a dignified harmonic rage   The future is a door with things behind it we must imagine
          In my alley, no one fucks with girls   We fuck you up with halogen hand job bombs
Thread thick steel screws in your tires to let out all that life

/

I have so many devices for your self-sentenced death

/

I took a class and learned to swim: upside down, to dive, to hold my breath and get across

This isn't a fake ass Atlantis with Godzilla hieroglyphics   This new home I made for us is
Gojira's neutron breath, a new life to light the sky with
          This weapon is my memory: a mí no se me olvida nada

/

Cyanotype (in a New York Public Library)

The amount of work that Anna Atkins—with the help of her servants—
had to do over the years to produce
British Algae should not be underestimated

How do you press the earth into a book?
Glass planes turn salty sea plants into hair fractures
A carrot top with a sun in its heart
Chestnuts with looping tails
A feathered wig for a Who

Here I am, dredging up olive trees
underneath a sky painted on the ceiling
A window-laden room
The most beautiful thing, the most beautiful sound
is a library full of silent readers. Wooden chairs scrape
the floor. The occasional cough. Pages being turned, my hands
covered in topaz

The leaves might stick if they are too mucousy
and then there is no image to reveal. Miss Anna
Which are your ideas and which were someone else's?
What is your work and what is someone's life?
What is your hobby and what is my survival?

Servants are scientists and actors
Here is me pretending to be interested in sea trash
Here is me instructing my maiden on her indigo backwash

In the Amazon there is still war
In the name of cleansing, we burn palo santo
which are our ancestors. We rob them of their shade for good

The Santa Ynez mountains are ablaze with temperature and powerlines
And yet, the stolen water and grass baskets
found the last family who knows their songs

I turned another page of azure and old debuts
This one is missing its jellyfish tentacles
That one is a wiry white beard

Comadre, I don't know what to tell you
We are with you, in different cages, tipping into a new page
Here is a spade, a roof. Flat grasses and two almonds

If Guinea fowl feathers could speak for themselves they'd want
a future of playing in violet sheets and daylight
Polka Dot feathers and tiaras made of amethyst

Hydrolytic tendency means I have a mildly acidic condition
So I guess I am a sour ass motherfucker

A servant in service to my writing, I'm an electron
of this marble, a sedimental lion if there ever was one
Eyeshadow on this place from now on

At 4 a.m., the radio is off

There is no music I want to hear
When I drop off Pops at his job
I tuned him out, finally, and watch the road instead

City of Industry, the City of Commerce: temple warehouses of
shipping and receiving. Black lunchpails and blue cream cleanser
And a work ethic I'll never have

I drive home after leaving him there, wish if that's where he could stay
A stray bullet lodged in other mens' sleep and not ours
I double back on the 60 to sleep another hour
then will get myself to work 30 minutes east of East
My 9 to 5 of hallways wallpapered with temporary restraining orders
Yet my arm on the bench seat is still, like freedom

What does it feel like to drive my father's car?

Like a Coors Light that never got opened.
Like my stinging eyelids closing and my guts reopening
Like instead of smashing into the divider
I will take the Impala to court

There I will show it the mimeograph
How I record death threats and secrets
How the body deserves anything but this

I am giving the blue sky of its chrome another chance to live right,
to show my father and so many men like him to leave
women and girls the fuck alone. I do this before the Impala wrecks
for the last time, and I tumble out on my feet
I do it before the body disintegrates into the 18-wheeler
it will end up under, a hidden star exploding
into a galaxy it never knew it could be

It Is Winter and You're No Bunny Slope

I planted a Japanese maple in Oakland once
It's the only part of that house that still belongs to me

Is that smoke or are you just happy?
Peppermint stripes become you and
Alpine forests grow over at the right
altitude. They are not called pine trees here
Perhaps they are pinos

This looking is a gift
It was the beginning of summer when you jumped
from the couch to the mountains, from the ocean sand to volley up
to the sun, a striped ball
Then a sailboat slowly tipped to one side
without you noticing

This is an advertisement for vacations
and bathing suits that go down past your thighs
Very proper, very lady
Everything you have to say can be said sideways
and backwards. Just be careful
Remember the pale powder sky and that I
will be here next season

And where, my dear, will you be? Still mad because I got cuter shoes
Me, I'm on this black lacquered floor, safely tucked into a pocket

There is a net between us and time. Our countries are white lines traced
across our outfits, our passports
I am waiting for someone to tell me to get up
To stop, to go down the stairs and into
another silent room
Ah, there she is. She walked over to the balcony
and glanced at me. A warning

So I get up

And notice there are people that you will meet

once you arrive at the ski lodge

They wear yellow and blue

Power pink and purple pants

The trees are alpines but they are cerulean not _____

My seeing was off (this time)

Somewhere the Ainu are not skiing

From here it is impossible to see that they exist

It is just you and I and hidden hot springs. Hidden people

Who you sacrificed for a black clean floor

Overheard in a Garden

A mother tells her son to wait alone, outside of the orbit. He pouts. Looks inside the metal. He was being naughty. So he waited, what else. Now they're holding hands and that's it— that was the whole fight. And then they have repair. Things don't stay broken. Their nature is ornamental

I've never asked nature for answers, only miracles. That our children may escape any cages as photons or pollen: dispersible, untakeable

That's what I asked and the robles brushed. The polka dot finch zizzed. Not everything means something. Sometimes an answer is more questions and a rejection of your imposition

One sound inside me is a giant dripping faucet. Another is an ice cream cone melting

How many household items did those women in the Parisian book insert? Candles. A skinny chair leg. The stem of an alcatraz, the most natural thing to put inside yourself. That way, you are growing something from within. My insides are Valerian. Peonies and willow.

My brother rolls mom's wheelchair into a short, wire volcano, its frame threaded with passion fruit vines. A spray of water mists her face. It's so hot that she sighs, Qué rico. Vente, she tells my husband. He smiles from outside the explosion. I am glad we all can fit in here.

Here, My Photo of You

For Shirin Neshat

You are nearly smiling. I apologize: I don't have a violin to accompany me

     I have tubas, snare drums, and men declaring seduction through their noses

It was time to go when the ocean herself took me by the legs

     and tumbled my ass out onto the shore. And now we are back, to the beach

where this began—there are so many ways to go home again

     Let it come to you in the atoms of rosewater. In the turmeric

of the tongue. Crumbled over firozeh and the sweetness of your son's hands

     Here are the waves: blue-green that swell and never crash

They grow and grow, passing you from one hand to the next

     until you are in the center of the sea

We know what it's like not to go home. Neither here nor there, we

     made home in the middle. What is madness but another way to see the world

To survive that which otherwise kills us on the inside and in real life

     What is madness but the way we crack misogyny with the butt of a rifle

Mexika Hi Fem (Coatlicue Come)

After Rafa Esparza and Celia Herrera Rodriguez

My offering to the world is this bloody maw. I watch the live feed from your pupils. This is all that's left of my land. But I have returned to claim all of my thrones. I am hungry for myself, for the children I have made and now must devour, lest you invent them into something they are not. Me crees cruel porque te digo la verdad. Pero yo no soy la que siente. La que sufre. Yo hago y deshago. Muelo violadores y me los trago. I am. Still. Hungry. Tell me what you are, not what you think. This is ceremony and I want you to dance. Yo no conozco países y mapas. Yo sé. Yo soy. Yo soy dos serpientes y siempre cambio. Tiene mucho rato que no comía. Qué te parecen mis ligas negras. Mis deseos: bailes en lo oscuro. Uñas doradas. Qué tal estas trenzas. The first thing you see is the neon so you know that we are in the present or the future. I don't fuck with linear time. The end is a Reggaeton soundtrack and my laughter. El neón rosa y morado, mis pezuñas. Ya llego por quien llorabas. Quema tu copal que no va quedar nada. Throw me the Baby Jesús, he's my desayuno. Ahórrate el sermón. Esto es todo lo que queda de mi tierra. Cómo crees que me sentí cuando llegaron y me nombraron otra cosa. First I will eat San Juanita de los Lagos. Tus pestañas son tan reales. Femininity is my top, my favorite snack. Tus labios me saben a yeso. Of gold-laced robes. Demasiado lágrimas y más sangre. Ahórrate tu despecho que a los santos no les duele. Que se te olvidó quiénes son realmente? El aire. Tu espíritu. El fuego. I am not who you think I am. I will always exist—in your grind—in the temple—in the very water and clay that makes everything you build with me. It's your turn to feast, my serpent children. Eat these police cars, these Dixie farms, this excuse for matricide. I love all of the screaming. The museum is too quiet. And this music makes me want to bring the rest of my body back to life. Lo que no se destruye es el significado. Qué te parece mi nuevo cuerpo, mis tatuajes.

Mis amantes who tie my black harness, my scales
turned to skin. I am no monster. I trust myself.
In the beginning, in the end. *Confío en*
mí Yo merezco respeto. Me quiero
a mi misma. Respiro. Observo
Procedo. Esta es ceremonia
y vamos a bailar. Here is
the drum again –
Ahí   – Ahí   – Ahí
Love me like the
Virgen, like your
sins, and just
let me eat
you

Notes

Epigraphs: The excerpt from Adrienne Rich's poem is my way of linking my first poetry collection to this one. There, the last poem is titled "Out of the Wreck," after Rich's "The Stranger." Here we begin with and through the idea of a wreck, the body of an accident, and what is left after a collision.

In their essay "the university: last words," an ongoing conversation continued from their *The Undercommons: Fugitive Planning and Black Study*, written for/through the Fuck UC graduate student action network's online symposium, July 9, 2020, Fred Moten and Stefano Harney invoke C. L. R. James, a Black historian, intellectual, journalist, and socialist, who wrote: "I am a black man number one, because I am against what they have done and are still doing to us; and number two, I have something to say about the new society to be built because I have a tremendous part in that which they have sought to discredit." I am grateful for, indebted to, and aim to be in conspiracy with radical Black Thought, which always expands the multiple dimensions of creativity and possibility for all of us.

"nature armed medicine": This is an erasure and remix of The Treaty of Guadalupe Hidalgo and Juan Gabriel's song "La Farsante." The Nahuatl phrases are from the poem "Tu Chalchi-huite Se Va" by Alfredo Ramírez C., translated by E. Fernando Nava L. in "Siete Poemas en Náhuatl de Xalitla, Guerrero," an excerpt from the magazine *UNAM Instituto de Investigaciones Históricas*, circa 1986: http://www.historicas.unam.mx/publicaciones/revistas/nahuatl/pdf/ecn19/319.pdf.

"Umbral": After Nicanor Parra and W. Miller's translations of "Memorias de juventud" in Nicanor Parra's *Antipoems: New and Selected*, edited by David Unger (New York: New Directions, 1985).

"Only We Make Beautiful Things Just to Destroy Them": After the video in the exhibition *La Gravedad de los Asuntos (Matters of Gravity)* by The Arts Catalyst's zero gravity programme, as installed in the Museum of Latin American Art, Long Beach, California, in 2019.

"'69 Chevy Impala": I grew up in a home where my father was always buying old cars, fixing them in the driveway, on the side of the road, or taking photos of himself next to cars he wanted or borrowed. Classic cars meant he'd look good, be noticed by other car lovers, but they were also a vehicle to hunt in. The problem was that every single car he ever owned was busted, not unlike his intentions. I want to make something, anything else out of that.

"I don't know what else to tell you about t e a r g a s": The former deputy chief of the U.S. Border Patrol and 2019 president of the Border Patrol Foundation said this about using tear gas on refugees in Tijuana: "To clarify, the type of deterrent being used is OC pepper spray. It's literally water, pepper, with a small amount of alcohol for evaporation purposes." He continued, "It's natural. You could actually put it on your nachos and eat it. So it's a good way of deterring people without long-term harm." I refuse to name him.

"Anther": After the performance at Los Angeles Contemporary Exhibitions by Sebastian Hernández in Freewaves's *LOVE &/OR FEAR: A Celebration of Genders*, September 7, 2019.

"God Is a Jacket Made of Tinsel": After the film *A Fantastic Woman*. The line "Bájate cabrón que tengo una emergencia" is taken directly from the film. The words "bruised camellias" and "hologram" are inspired by Rocío Carlos' unpublished poem "harrow."

"La Cuenta": This poem is a Bop, a Black poetic form invented by Afaa Michael Weaver and originating in the United States. The italicized words are taken from the song "La Tracalera" by Johnny Herrera and performed by Selena. The phrase "We are only as good as the worst of our people" is from Cherríe Moraga, who wrote the play *Who Killed Yolanda Saldívar?* Thank you, Rocío Carlos, for naming this poem sin querer.

"Desfile": Of note regarding the technical Spanish spellings of words in this poem is that some follow what the Real Academia Española (RAE) would require using and some do not. In my first book, I actively resisted this kind of correction. With this book, I reached out to my friend and translator JD Pluecker to conspire about what is "right" and what to update so that I may be clearly understood. In an email, JD wrote this about the "suggestions" to this poem: ". . . the RAE guidelines change all the time. and i am no RAE editing expert either. and as i mention in one comment, there is *thankfully* no Chicano/x/e/a RAE so you can def do whatever you want." In helping me update this poem and others with Spanish in it, JD noted that "anyone who sees something as 'error' is saying more about themselves and their formation than about you and your poems, honestly. all of these things are so weird and complicated and whatever decision you make is great IMHO." Therefore, "América" in this poem is spelled

"America" because the newscaster in the poem pronounced it incorrectly as "Uh-meh-rih-cuh." He said it incorrectly because people of the global majority would pronounce it América, and so, to tip those scales more toward what it true than what dominates, I must leave it "wrong." It's a textual revenge. While we are here, América is two continents, not one country. Please make a note, ya estuvo suave.

"Disco": After Circus Disco, Totó La Momposina's song "La Verdolaga," and Rocío Dúrcal. The words "Como copo de algodón, ay la verdolaga" are lyrics from Totó La Momposina's song.

"I('m) a dominó, every here": This is an erasure of the poem "Anecdote of the Jar" by Wallace Stevens who called Gwendolyn Brooks a racial slur when she was awarded the Pulitzer Prize.

Also, the RAE got rid of the accented versions of the word "esa" and "ese." However, because in some ways I am fighting the RAE and other English or corrected conventions of language, I left the accent in "ése" because here the accent is a portable knife of self-determination. [Stab stab].

"Happiness Is Going to Pieces": After Victor Estrada's sculpture, *Happiness*, 1994–1995, foam, plaster, and paint, 78x77x34in, Museum of Contemporary Art, Los Angeles, https://www.moca.org/artist/victor-estrada.

"I Want to Last": The italicized words are from Tracy K. Smith's poem "Flores Woman." The line "a mighty long time" was an unconscious echo of and influenced by Prince's lyrics in "Let's Go Crazy."

"Do You Know What Time It Is?": After the photograph *Candy Cigarette* by Sally Mann and the protest-performance organized by Cherríe Moraga and Celia Herrera Rodriguez with the non-profit Al Otro Lado at the Otay Mesa Detention Center. This facility gives detainees a fifteen-minute break per day, in the confines of a tall-walled balcony. They are able to see about seven by seven feet of sky and nothing more. This poem is dedicated to them. To support the work of Al Otro Lado, who collects the testimonies of and supports people in detention, literally picking people up once they are released, visit https://alotrolado.org. To see the photograph, visit https://www.mocp.org/detail.php?t=objects&type=related&kv=2380.

"La Corona": This poem is in response to and in conversation with the TV series *The Crown*, the women in my family, and a conversation on colonialism, the pandemic, and the home between Cherríe Moraga and Celia Herrera Rodriguez. The words "living in the shadow of the Mission" were Celia's as the pandemic shut down a lot of activity in California. The conversation was called "Conversaciones de Sobremesa: La Madre Has Mounted the Defense Troops," accessed on April 25, 2020 at https://mcusercontent.com/cec26e75554daae23bf 293c0a/files/1420c401-5cf1-44b0-bdf0-839e9f1faf61/REV._Sobre_Mesa_1.March_22_4 _25_20_6.57_PM.mp3. The conversation is archived with Las Maestras Center for Xicana[x] Indigenous Thought, Art and Social Praxis at UC Santa Barbara.

"'85 Chevy El Camino": After Rose B. Simpson's *Maria* in honor of artist Maria Martinez. The italicized words are from an interview Simpson gave to the Denver Art Museum about her work in the 2013 show, "Sovereign: Independent Voices." The poem follows Simpson's performance and installation of the car into the Denver Art Museum, but it also documents the procession of queer Native people in futuristic clothing the artist designed and handmade.

"Thank You 1-800#s": After Ross Gay's poem "To My Best Friend's Big Sister."

"Still—Each and Every": This is an erasure of the poem "Cacoethes Scribendi," by Oliver Wendell Holmes, Sr.

"I'm that bitch: A Voice Mail": During *RuPaul's Drag Race*, season 11, Vanessa "Vanjie" Mateo and Brooke lynn Hytes had a work room romance. During the reunion episode, however, when asked if they were still an item, Vanjie said "I wanted *The Notebook* experience, and I was getting a Post-It." I decided to write her in my own drag persona.

"Three Girls in a Subway": After an unnamed photograph of three young Black women on a subway taken by photographer Michael A. McCoy. See photograph at https://blackshutter-podcast.com/the-black-shutter-podcast/ep-7-michael-a-mccoy.

"We Had to Become Doves: An American Sonnet": This poem is an American sonnet, a Black U.S. American poetic form reinvented by Wanda Coleman. The poem is written after select images and film stills in Shirin Neshat's exhibition at the Broad, Los Angeles, *Shirin Neshat: I Will Greet the Sun Again* and its photography installation *The Home of My Eyes*, and Shahrnush Parsipur's *Women Without Men: A Novel of Modern Iran*.

"Jotería [All the things you forgot to say]": After the excerpt of Deborah Richards's "Reading Aloud: An Intimate Performance (2015)" in *Letters to the Future: Black Women/Radical Writing*, edited by Erica Hunt and Dawn Lundy Martin (Tucson: Kore Press, 2018). "What is hidden from the wise and good" is taken directly from Richards's text. The line "Even elision makes a sound," is from Tisa Bryant's essay "*from* Our Whole Self An Intraview of Black Women Writers' Experimentation Essay on Elided African Diasporic Aesthetics in Prose" in Hunt and Martin's *Letters to the Future*. Mexican drag queen Margaret Y Ya said, "Yo me sentí muy perra." My mom said "Hay que tener maña. Y yo soy mañosa." Mexicanness via mestizaje and José Vasconcelos's "La Raza Cósmica" is a story told through white supremacy that many of us have believed, we are so desperate to love ourselves. To read further about this project, see Tanya Katerí Hernández, "'Too Black to be Latino/a': Blackness and Blacks as Foreigners in Latino Studies," *Latino Studies* 1:1 (March 2003): 152–59, and chapter 2 of Hernández, *Racial Subordination in Latin America The Role of the State, Customary Law, and the New Civil Rights Response* (Cambridge: Cambridge University Press, 2012). I also recommend Alan Pelaez Lopez's essay, "The X in Latinx Is a Wound, Not a Trend," Color Bloq, September 2018, https://www.colorbloq.org/the-x-in-latinx-is-a-wound-not-a-trend.

"Here, My Photo of You": Zora Neale Hurston wrote "I couldn't see it [my garment] for wearing it" in the introduction to Hurston, *Mules and Men*.

"Mexika Hi Fem (Coatlicue Come)": After Rafa Esparza's performance of the same name at the Traición festival in Mexico, 2018. In collaboration with Lady Soul Fly, assisted by Sebastian Hernandez, Rafa performed in elegant harnesses in his recreated face of Coatlicue, the Mexica/Nahua serpent mother destroyer. The phrase "This is all that's left of my land" is taken from Celia Herrera Rodriguez's performance "Cositas Quebradas" in Málaga, Spain, where, inside a church, she smashed their patron saint to pieces. The text and italics is from a photograph taken by writer and photographer Marisela Norte. In one of Norte's photos, a painting is bolted to a bus stop shelter and in the painting, a pre-Columbian figure speaks these words of affirmation and self-love in Spanish: "*Confío en mí, Yo merezco respeto. Me quiero a mi misma. Respiro. Observo. Procedo.*"

VICKIE VÉRTIZ

is an award-winning Mexican American poet, writer, and professor whose work has appeared in the *New York Times* magazine, the *San Francisco Chronicle*, and the *Los Angeles Review of Books*. Her book *Palm Frond with Its Throat Cut* won the 2018 PEN America literary prize in poetry. A graduate of Williams College, the University of Texas at Austin, and the University of California, Riverside, she teaches in the Writing Program at UC Santa Barbara.